LUNAR ECLIPSE

THE ANTHOLOGY OF EMERGING EMOTIONS & REVOLUTIONS OF LOVE

THE GODDESS ANAHATA

LUNAR LEVELS PUBLISHING

LUNAR LEVELS PUBLISHING LLC
P.O. Box 19184
Louisville, KY USA

www.lunarlevelspub.com
outreach@lunarlevelspub.com
socials: @mahogany.speakspoetry
@lunarlevelspublishing

Cover Art/Design: Mahogany M. Shelton
Author Photograph: Mahogany M. Shelton
Illustrations: Mahogany M. Shelton

ISBN: 979-8-218-24004-2

Printed in the United States of America

Para mi familia de cuatro y más momentos.
Para que te entiendas a ti mismo.
Escribí este libro con amor.

ॐ

Mahogany Speaks

POETRY

THE

GODDESS
AHAHATA

CONTENTS:

INTRODUCING

In the grand tapestry of existence, poetry stands as the pinnacle of artistry, a malleable testament to the limitless bounds of imagination. It is the elusive chameleon of language, its form and color ever-changing, its essence as fluid as the river of time itself. In a world locked within the confines of three dimensions, we often find ourselves trapped in the binary coding of its two-dimensional framework. Yet, our souls yearn for a transcendent connection - a quintessential bond with our true selves, the palpable reality, and the unseen supra-realism that reverberates only in the chambers of emotions.

To navigate the labyrinth of love is to master the journey of life. From the raw, juvenile stirrings of the heart to the refined, mature grasp of realism, the pieces nestled in this anthology serve as a temporal voyage, a distillation of myriad moments into a single, pulsating blip of existence.

Amid the cacophony of modern life, serenity unveils itself when we emancipate our minds from the societal shackles. It invites us to relinquish the heart and mind's low vibrational frequencies and ascend to the plane of Chi, that sacred realm of harmony, akin to the teachings of Ma'at and Taoism.

To love, and be loved rightly, is to quell the tempest of chaos and birth a new reality from the ashes of the old. Love, both a conscious decision and an inexorable destiny, is guided by our perception and perspective. Each line within these pages springs forth from authentic emotions and revelations, from profound interactions and love, from undeniable truths and dreams, from heartfelt yearnings and the cognitive artistry of the mind.

Like the lunar eclipse, these verses symbolize a divine alignment- Earth poised between Sun and Moon, a beautiful reflection of the convergence of mind, body, and transcendental spirit. Here, in the stillness of this celestial harmony, the essence of life is to be discovered- an exquisitely balanced dance of divinity, beauty, melodic harmony, and omnipotent love. It is a ceaseless revolution, an endless cycle of death and rebirth, a timeless waltz guided by the eternal rhythm of the cosmos.

Here, you will encounter the eclectic web of human experience and, in the process, uncover the sophisticated elegance of life's most profound truths. With each verse, you are invited to partake in this timeless dance of wisdom and wonder. Asé.

"Ne basez pas ma intelligence uniquement sur ma performance sur papier, mais sur ma capacité à la partager avec le monde et à créer quelque chose de la belle."

PLEASING

• ONE NIGHT •

YOUR SKIN ON MY SKIN
WITHOUT HESITATION, I DIVE IN.
NOTHING EVER TASTED AS LOVELY
AS THE INTOXICATING SWEETNESS
OF YOUR MELANIN.

NO WORDS EXCEPT MY MOANS
AND YOUR WHISPERS IN MY EAR.
ALL THAT'S BEEN GONE SO LONG
HAS FINALLY REAPPEARED.

GOOSEBUMPS ON YOUR NECK
CHILLS ALL ON MY THIGH,
NEVER KNEW HOW YOU COULD FEEL SO GOOD
AND NOW YOU FINALLY KNOW WHY.

LISTENING TO SADE
YOU GET HIGHER AS YOU CARESS MY CURVES,
HERE WE ARE MAKING POETRY
INSTRUMENTAL WITH NO WORDS.

HOLD ME STRONG,
STROKE ME GENTLE,
I'M IN YOUR HEAD,
YOU'RE IN MY MENTALS.

NOW'S THE TIME, BALLADS PLAYING
SEEING STARS, ON A CLOUD;
SENSES COMMUNICATING, HEAR WHAT THEY SAYING
WHO KNEW A SMILE COULD BE SO LOUD?

THIS LITTLE INFINITY
EVER SO TENDERLY
YOU LOVING MY WAVE
I ADMIRE YOUR ENERGY.

IN THIS MOMENT RIGHT HERE
COMPLETELY IN HEAVEN
NOW WE'RE INSEPARABLE
AFTER A ROUND... OR ELEVEN.

● my strange addiction ●

i think i'm addicted

to the masculine energy.

being the only female

form in sight to admire

the pulchritude

of divine masculine halo.

i take in the intoxicating aroma

and become

high.

the sight behold makes

my eyes dance-

entranced by the wave

of pure male essence.

being the one to grace

my femininity in the air

and waltz throughout the room.

i'm addicted to the

masculine energy.

inhaling it all

breath by breath.

• r & r •

You turn me on

Like a moth to a flame

Like a junkie to the pain

Like a desert with some rain

                    I just need it

Like some laces on a shoe

Like the sky loves blue

Like a "bless you" to an achoo

                    It just makes sense

And it might sound a little silly

But i just want you to know really

That you ain't gotta be touchy feely

                    To get me hot

Your voice is like a song

That lets me know where i belong

From night until dawn

                    You're on my body

I deeply breathe you in

Engulfed in your melanin

Just show me where to begin

                    Volume up

And let me not get distracted

Can't help how i'm acting

Got my soul doing backflips

                  No off button

Fragrance so light

With an aura so bright

Your smile lights up the night

                  My shooting star

Warrior so gallant

We'll build our own palace

Your sword, my magic

                  Impenetrable creation

Say love, you turn me on

Like a flash to the dark

Like a joint's first spark

Like insanity's work of art

                  Good all over

Mind, body, spirit

Can't you tell i feel it

All my prayers and wishes

                  Were answered all along

● Can You; I Will ●

I wouldn't dare change a thing if I could do it over thrice.
I look at you and daydream just so I could see you twice.

Is that a smile I see in the cracks of your sadness?
Come ride my vibration; here's your invitation.
Can you be the rhythm to my blues? And the wind in my hips?
How about the gravity that catches me when I grind then dip?
I hear what you don't say baby, words are overrated.
Can I ride your vibration? Where's my invitation?
Together we can be a song- my melody and your beat.
I'm the groove your restless hands been waiting to come meet.
Let those gypsy eyes greet these gypsy thighs.
Time in stillness, so we got all night.
Can the warmth from you make a chill in me?
Will the way you move find my spot of ecstasy?
You'll get lost in the sea of me baby, is that alright with you?
I just wanna make you... *shhh* and you make me... *don't speak* The
passion from your rhythm makes me oh so weak.
I see you when I close my eyes.
It's on repeat when I awake.

I wouldn't dare change a thing if I could do it over thrice.
I look at you and daydream just so I could see you twice.

Now tell me one more time love, is that alright with you?
Can your lips make my shoulders shake?
Can you taste my sweet surrender?
Can you feel my knees make the ground quake?
I'll receive if you're my sender.
I will mend your sadness and stitch it with a smile.
I hope you're not in a hurry, baby it's gon' be a while.
I will make your back my trophy, scarred with my prize.
Even bare, I will still undress you with my gypsy eyes.

Come to me love,
and let's make this love making a time to make love make itself

infinite.

● Control Me ●

make me submit to you
only for you
tell me hold my climax
until you say word
even when i beg
force me to hang on
and with your permission
i'll release

• Canvas •

Paint me. For I am your canvas.
I am an unfinished work of art, but have never been blank.
With each stroke, guide me, for you are the paintbrush
and beauty is in the eye of the beholder. But don't
correct my misshapen lines. Add to
them: more path, more road,
more track to discover
as I uncover the
art I back at.
Two roads diverged by a painter's brush and I, I took the one that
traveled straight to your heart and found peace to let my paint
dry. There is no way to correctly interpret the euphoric
sensation I get when you paint me paintbrush-
try bliss. Paint on me the goodness in
your soul and what you'd never
want to take back. For I
am your canvas and
beauty is in the eye of
the beholder.
Just don't let me crack unkempt when you're stuck. The paintbrush must
paint as love demands to be felt. The canvas must be painted as a
bird longs to fly. Make me like Mona Lisa with your
velvet paint and unlock a new masterpiece.

● Tea Time ●

I lit up when you spoke about crystals and astronomy.

Eyes got big as you showed me your Qi Gong techniques.

My ears danced hearing the physics of life and ontological mathematics.

And when you made those herbs into a tea for me...

that's when it all exploded.

Mix the maca root with the tongkat ali. Might as well be Muhammad Ali,

with all that force, the way you shaking my maraca.

Extra sweet on the menu please?

Liquid butterscotch on caramel rocks.

Take a sip of that.

Timeless aphrodisiac.

No holding back.

Don't let me go. My Shango.

Now tell me more. Show me how you lead your woman.

● hot ice   cold honey ●

Let me warm my hands on you and melt on to your skin.
*Palms disappearing into you *breathe*.*
I am how honey,
Hydrating your DNA with the sticky glaze of my sweet sugar.
*I can taste you- magically gliding across my lips with each kiss *mmm*.*
I'm getting warmer.
Heating up- creating a new shade of Mahogany.
How on earth did I get here? All the way to my melting point and I'm
stuck. I don't know if X or G should mark the spot. But I'm hot now; and
all it takes is an embrace to seize the day and make you mine. The
polarity of our hearts interlaced whispering the secrets of boundless
enchantment. Say everything I just can't.

Preocupado contigo mí amor.
Too busy making your vessel glow- illuminating ambiance of the gods.
Speak to the heavens and profess the lullaby of vibrating melanin
*dancing together mixing honeycomb with magic *breathe*. Take me to*
the sun, transfixed into a beautiful shape I call {this}.
Siempre juntos.

• CLOUDS OF AWE •

ARE YOU MY LOVE? YO NO SÉ.

BUT WHAT I DO KNOW IS THIS:

I'M IN AWE WITH THIS EXPERIENCE AND I'D BE
REMISS IF I DIDN'T PROCLAIM IT TO THE WORLD.

TO BE A BEE FINDING THE PERFECT
FLOWER, EAGER TO TELL THE HIVE ITS STORY, THAT'S ME.

TO BE THE SAHARA'S SINGLE OASIS AND THE
CAMEL OF TWELVE THOUSAND MILES, THAT'S ME.

TO FEEL THE WEIGHTLESSNESS THAT IS
FLOATING, FALLING, AND FLYING, THAT'S ME.

I'M IN AWE WITH THIS EXPERIENCE BECAUSE I FEEL
YOU FEELING ME IN A WAY THAT ONLY SOUNDLESS SPACE
COULD DESCRIBE. THE OXYGEN IN YOUR BLOOD BRINGS ME
TO LIFE. IN THE BOTTOM OF THE WISHING WELL, WE CAN
BREATHE NOW. DECADENT CLUSTERS OF PRAYER
FOREVERMORE.

● don't make it hard ●

maybe one day

you will finally see

that I was always right here.

• ramble •

i got higher than the stars last night and thought about you.

when i was up, i wanted to take them with me on the way down.

but i can't keep all the light to myself; too much love among the galaxies.

i visited my favourite star and we talked about you.

it sounded like a cool ocean breeze- no turbulence -

just a gentle admiration.

● There's Lunch OUTSIDE ●

It's a lovely day
today
if I do so say ---

And if I may... for a second, paint a picture:

Under a secluded tree,
sun twinkling through the leaves,
harvesting nature's remedy, you sit with her.

Now you're a little hungry, but your brain gets fuzzy,
because you can't tell where the fruit basket ends and she begins.

So you have both.

You ever bite into
a piece of dragon fruit
while she's draggin' her fruit
back and forth on you?
A perfect symbiosis of secrets dripping from your chin,
dopamine and oxytocin,
everything all at once.
Time to taste the mango,
same time she hangs low,
surfing your body;
expanding & contracting as you intake that double dose of sugar.

Now put the seeds near the roots,
full from juice of all the fruits.
A new experience for you, one to savour.

Evidence of a sweet farewell. A secret only the tree can tell.
Enjoying Mother Nature's fairytales,
When's the next time?

ride the wave of my hips like water
feel the frequency in how we pulsate together.
gift and guidance from Oshun- goddess of love, beauty, and the moon
all encapsulated in this one vessel for you to digest
and the rest completes itself.
your fire to my ice
releasing my inner secrets of conquest into the flame the propels them.
ride the wave of my hips like water
tilting east and west with pure passion making
the oceans rock together.
slide into my darkness while i come into your light
conductive. energetic. intensely magnetic.
electric light. add electrolytes to this new shape of water-
submerged in the fountain of youth.
entranced in the flow of where i take you
cleansed mind transformed into kinetic radiance.
speak love into me
whisper into my crystals all of your good intentions
and witness how they form.
it only takes one; necesitas bailar conmigo ahora.

● ...When In Rome ●

...and then he grinned at me and asked this: "Who are you?"

as if a genie granted him a wish he forgot to ask.

with no words, my aura touched his to respond, "the mystery and answer,

soil that grows the fruit, fire to keep your soul warm; the one and only"

a binaural hemisync of simplicity where love and logic live lucidly.

"Where did you come from?" he inquired

waiting for it to be less real.

so my eyes said this: "the wind and sea, sent from ancient willow trees,

here to help you make your dreams come true".

in our final embrace, desire danced on my fingertips.

where the sweetest kiss almost lived, tension grew in the longing

for submission to his lips, my calmness draped in silk.

flow frolicked freely between us two... that's when he knew.

● Only a T-Shirt ●

She's been waiting,
in quiet anticipation
underneath that XL tee
to get him exactly
in position.
In shadows cast by candle's soft illumination,
her form, a sculpture of caramel smoothness;
a silent invitation, quiet in the dimmed room, an intimate taunt.
Lips that sing.
smooth as silk, he's captivated; lulled into rhythms guiding his every
movement. The soft cadence of her words- gentle nudge to explore the
sanctuary nestled within her essence.
Lips that call.
She lures the Tree of Life closer, closer
until he reaches heaven's gates forming a velvet trail to the hidden
paradise where dimensions dissolve, here in between.
She wants him to lift the curtain,
reveal the stage.
His desire, a beacon, piercing through the veil of the night. An intimate
map to the cosmos, drawn in the language of twilight. Her touch, a map
etched in passion on the ridges of his back and sealed with a sigh, guides
him up the celestial ladder. A right of passage is met.
Door is open, passcode spoken
in the hushed whispers between two souls unbroken;
sensual ecstasy. They never knew stars could make love.

Underneath her XL tee,
the swell of her breasts rise and fall to the rhythm of her heart -
a seductive drumbeat in his ear. Each curve a constellation as he
navigates down to Orion's Belt.
His rod, his staff, manhood, his shaft, it comforts her.
On their California King, bodies meld, his sacral chakra surges, and
boundaries blur between carnal and ethereal. Waves of energy spiral
upwards, reaching the crown, and ripple outwards, coursing through
dimensions unfathomable.
A new portal is created.
After a day spent shaping the world, touching lives, and stirring hearts,
they find solace in this intimate space. they bare their vulnerabilities. In
this unguarded moment, in this shared silence, they foster love -
transformative.

LOVING

• time warp •

I love you from Earth's core to the oldest living star.

I am the softness in your lips and the unwind in your mental.
The only way to describe my passion for you is for you to place your
hand upon my chest.

Do you feel each beat spelling the letters in your name?
How the blood rushes to your hand for each nerve to sense the energy
flow from me to you?

Can you feel me wash away your insecurities?
You see my soul smile bigger and shine brighter than the laugh of a baby
or the sun after a storm.

If you remove your hand from my heart, you'll still feel it
pulsating in your palm.
Bond stronger than chemistry, force breaking all laws of physics.

I've already thought of a hundred ways to make you smile.
Rest your weary head on my shoulder and I'll start with number one....

the intoxicating aroma. the strength in a hug. the curve of a smile. how the dimple won't hide any more. the fifty shades of brown. stress lines on the forehead. combination of smoothed callous hands to hold. the war scars lining the body. bass of voice based deep in choice. ears curved in curiosity. power push of the shoulders. the chest of a million breaths. a new found peace from the pain behind the eyes. command the room. step heavy. unconditional courage. many things about you enthrall me. just starting with your avatar. now can i see what's inside?

just one hug and my clothes smell like you. i couldn't get you out of my mind even if i tried because

you're already on my skin darlin. every time you're not around, you're still here.

i love you so bad that i'm addicted- the soothing pain of a first tattoo hurts so good- you can never have just one. i love you so vividly that i see you in my dreams even when i'm awake. what's it gonna take for you to understand a love in innocence so heaven sent? but i repent.

and i just love you so true that i would move the Earth for you and repaint the grass until it's purple and blue.

but maybe i do love you too much

because it hurts and such when you use previous mistrust to put my affection on a crutch and misuse it.

to you i will cater- sweet now and later, to be the fix of the left twix one bite and all the wrong turns right.

nothing you do could ever break or mistake this burning passion that i have to be loved by all your flaws. without man, there's no woman

you're the 'wow' in power, i'm the 'she' to your shine-

it starts and ends with me in you; giving me your heart and... showing you mine.

but maybe i do love you too much

because i just wanna cry all your lost tears take all your worst fears and be your little hurricane so that you can be happy again. what else do you need to see?

let me drop down to my knees— i love you i am yours and you are the one for me.

i love everything about you
and everything you come with
but the only "come" i don't need is
when you come to me and we...
get real nasty...
and start kissing all intimately...
and we know what would come next

but still, i just might love you too much

     sometimes it does suck
     but i don't feel it any less
     even with the stress
     you're still the best

every flavour of you is still my favourite
you make my heart gleam
the universe used pure moonlight to make you
no matter what my flower, i will find your soul in every lifetime so that i
may have the honor

               of loving you all over again

● First Love ●

they say that the first man a girl learns to love is her father.
well, i didn't get that luxury,
but there's this boy...

i remember the first time we met-
heart so big with a body so fragile. those big brown eyes and soft
charcoal hair- i was instantly in love. he had this button nose and
dazzling aura and i just knew that i'd always keep him safe. I found a
new purpose; i felt the flame in my soul in that moment with every fiber
of my being. he could have my right lung, both kidneys, and my left leg.
my body, his shield- i would always protect him.
his name: Jeremiah.

then i got to do it again...
because who really gets to have true love twice? but this one was
stubborn. he was always a fighter. he told me the first time we met that
things would always go his way. too beautiful to ever say NO to. he
would always be mine. i vowed to be
his warrior and his keeper. no greater pleasure on this earth than having
his love to hold for eternity.
his name: Joseph.

two loves for life.
two true beams of light.
for the rest of my existence.
learning from blood.
with them, i feel like a superhero; to learn how they need to be treated
and cared for is a privilege.

they say the first man a girl usually loves is her father...
i got the blessing of young brothers. my gentle giant and my wild card.
true at heart. i've been love struck.

● my sleep ●

When the melatonin kicks in,
The tone in my breaths become melodic;
Sweetly slumped into a soft serenade of signs and songs.

Eyes closed and I swim through a sea of scenes
Until I can find the message-
Wondering how the next rise will happen.

In that slumber you're there being you, letting us be us
And it's a moment of forever between: zero and one.

There's so much that can happen.

And when the melatonin wears off,
Remnants of recollection race and refuse to rest.

It's us all over again.

However long we're together doesn't matter to me
And I don't need to be asleep to see you in my dreams.

• DONUTS •

One can't be upset when saying or eating a donut-
it just sounds silly and there's no way it makes sense.
You are my donut.
Even when I'm pissed at you,
I smile again when your name runs across my lips.
The sweet glaze of each kiss reminds me
that there is no way I can stay mad at you.
Each bite of donut is better than the last-
hoping that it will never end
and that there's another in the box.
You are my donut.
So many flavours, just like your attitude.
While I may not like them all,
I still can't hate a single one.
I have you and we work together.
Even when you turn stale,
your glaze is still delicious
and I still know what (and who) you are.
You are my donut.
You've never lost value to me.
You only need a little warming up.
Even when I don't want to like you,
I still do. I always have. I love donuts.
Donuts make me happy.
The love I have for donuts is uniquely unmatched.
You are my donut.

• Weighted Streams •

It took time for me to embrace my tears as power with the weight they hold. They shaped me as does the water over rocks in streams; my offering to the spirit guides. A soul cleanse, a marvelous balance. Each tear serenades my cheeks a sad farewell, a pain that no longer lives inside. Released into the ether, the balance of water that is I, is restored.

• COLOURS •

right now is of the essence
and this is a little new
so please be patient if i don't get it all right
hidden interests and thoughts & a passion for life that's been lost
a light so bright may make others uncomfortable
don't ever forget me, but for now we have this moment, so look:

you a gangsta and i thank ya for all the laughs we've shared;
behind that nervous smile is the real you somewhere. every time
you almost show it, you bury it even deeper
fishing for the soul that cries out- hook, line, no sinker.
it's clear that you've been hurt before
like throwing salt on an open sore.
true love hasn't found you yet, so you won't let your heart love no more.
we all have our trust issues but let love find you, i implore.
magical- like a unicorn or a shooting star from up above,
with the right affection, ain't no limit to what you're capable of.
it hurts it hurts (i know too well) to neglect your feelings for so long
sometimes doubting worthiness since too many have loved you wrong
you starved the wolf you should have fed
and fed the one already full
that, in turn, has turned you into
a kamikaze invading a whirlpool.

sometimes dear one, i say with fact,
      it's okay to move on impulse;
there will always be hits and misses
like drinking Hennessy and playing ring toss.
      there's a feeling of purgatory that creeps up, that sneaks up
            when you try anything to feel something just to end up with
nothing except finishing at the start
just to start at where you end up.
      pain of the past living in your forehead lines
      the reality you've been ducking;
i hope one day you find the one who'll make love
that 7am all nighter love- more than just fucking.
      she'll kiss every tattoo a thousand times,
      hold you close and you'll feel sublime.
you'll reciprocate just like a mime
profess your affections and she'll call you "mine".

● Softer ●

Allow me to be soft for you. In my softness, you can rest.

In my sweetness, is your sugar backbone.

In my care, you are safe.

In my light, you can see.

In my darkness, you can dream.

In my home, you may unwind. In my labyrinth, you may imagine.

It's softer here, warmer here,

sweeter everywhere that I am near.

Let me be here for you.

And because you're always here for me, I'm delighted to BE for you.

LOVE.

NEVER STOP LOVING. SHARE LOVE. SPREAD LOVE.

LOVE DEEPLY AND SINCERELY. IF YOU'VE LOVED ONCE, LOVE AGAIN.

IF YOU HAVEN'T LOVED YET, PRAY THAT LOVE FINDS YOU SOME LIFETIME.

LOVE HARDER AND FASTER THAN YOU'VE EVER LOVED BEFORE. LOVE A THOUSAND TIMES OVER IF THAT'S WHAT IT TAKES.

LOVE

LOVE IS ONE OF THE FEW METAPHYSICAL CONNECTIONS WE CAN TAKE WITH US AS WE TRANSCEND FROM ONE REALM TO THE NEXT.

MARVEL AT LOVE. LOVE IS THE PROFOUND AESTHETIC OF ETERNITY. LOVE CANNOT HURT YOU.

LOVE IS GRAND. BE OPEN TO LOVE. BE OPEN TO RECEIVE LOVE. BE OPEN TO EXPERIENCE EVERYTHING LOVE CAN GIVE.

LOVE IS INFINITE. LOVE IS A GIFT. ALWAYS REMEMBER LOVE AND LOVE WILL BE RIGHT BY YOUR SIDE.

SHAPE AND MOLD LOVE. LOVE IS A BOOMERANG.

YOU ARE WORTH LOVE. EXPRESS YOUR LOVE. LOVING ONLY WITH THE INTENTION OF GIVING.

RIDE LOVE'S VIBRATION NO MATTER HOW FAST OR SLOW, LONG OR SHORT EACH WAVE LASTS.

LOVE WAXES AND WANES LIKE THE MOON- CHANGING, FORMING DIFFERENT COLOURS AND SHAPES

BUT ALWAYS THERE.

LOVE IS THE MAGIC YOU BELIEVED IN AS A CHILD. LOVE IS AN ADVENTURE.

PRACTICE LOVE LIKE PATIENCE. LOVE EVEN IF IT GETS HARD.

UNCONDITIONALLY.

● nouvelle ●

you make me happy in ways
that i still
have to find new words for

• DREAM COME TRUE •

SO DEAR, THE EXHILARATING SOFTNESS OF YOUR TOUCH.
SUBLIME CREATION.
A KISS SHARED IN EVERLASTING.
TOO SWEET- EVEN A HUMMINGBIRD CAN MISS.
NEVER MISTAKEN,
A SERENITY OF THE HIGHEST MOUNTAIN CREEK.
AS WE INTERLOCK, BODY AND SPIRIT,
I REALIZE A JUBILANT INFLICTION
AND YOU'RE THE ONLY ONE
I WANT TO KISS
FOR THE REST OF MY LIFE.

● a time in space ●

this is a loose love
a free love
a "not tied down to me" love
an ever expressive feel love
a here "cause you wanna be" love

where you can roam
through the woods and play in the shadows
drown your sadness and let it wash
away so the free soul
can float to the top
where you can just be, judgment
free, and suddenly you can now see
all that was meant to be
honest and open i am here
with you as your air and heart
beat, in the womb of a
love that can rebirth you

this is an open love
not a choking love
a soulful love
not a moment love
across all galaxies, a roaming love
fly now and this love flies with you

we are one with it all. but you, even more, are the earth beneath my feet.

my rock and my stability

so i don't fall forever

the one constant

that i

don't ever have to question

you are the mineral deep rooted

among the chaos

i want to be

exactly where

you are

and with you,

earth, fire, wind,

i want to go

everywhere

and let's do

everything.

• Elated •

Why do you hold me like that?
The way that you do-
The way that lets me know
You'll always be here
To keep me safe.

Why do you kiss me like that?
Passionately.
Softly.
In a way that I've
never been kissed before.

Why are you like that?
You know, like THAT.
Just BEAUTIFUL.
A beautiful brown god
Whose melanin glistens in a way
To where I couldn't even imagine.

And I love you.
But why you do that?
Why you make me love you
the way that I do?

I don't know.
But I love it.

• TKO •

benevolently grab my wrists to stop my final fight.
place my hands on your chest and settle into your spirit.
hold me so close, short breaths.
just found my air.
my crown like ivy around your fingertips
knees buckled
and now i've lost my footing.
the Ra to my Thoth.
left hook, locked in, irises reading my Isis
"i love you" is what you tell me
and like nothing I've ever felt.... I know you mean it.

● p.o.v. ●

Action, verb, or noun.
Love is not either or.
But a totality of all.

● BOUND TOGETHER ●

WE'LL SPIN TOGETHER-
LIKE TWO PLANETS ASIDE
ONE ANOTHER
IN THE SAME DIRECTION,
BUT SO FAST;
TOO FAST FOR OTHERS TO
SEE, YET SLOW ENOUGH FOR
US TO ENCASE EVERY DETAIL

HIDING

• maniac •

just keep loving me.
even when i don't wanna talk.
even when you want to know what's wrong so bad and i just want to tell you everything and pour my heart out to you but i just can't. wanting to fill up a tall glass with my emotions and pour it through your fingertips, but it just gets too hard because then i think that maybe there's a chance you'll stop loving me.

just keep loving me.
even when i fall back into my rooted insecurities and i feel like i'm not pretty enough or good enough or smart enough and i know all of these things aren't true and that i'm great so i'm at war with myself and screaming at my subconscious while just begging for it to stop because it's too loud and i want to crawl out of my skin, but i'm stuck here.

just keep loving me.
even when i'm too much to deal with sometimes. and i'm really weird and eccentric. and i'm speaking clearly but in clear metaphors. so you still get confused about my message then misread it and don't want to understand or hear what i'm saying. even when i beg and plead my intentions but i come off aggressive and it's just gone too far left and i don't know what else to do but to retreat within myself and try to imagine how i'll be okay without you. but i could never be okay without you. I'm strong by myself but we're unstoppable together and it would hurt too bad to fathom you giving my love to anyone else if i can't have some too.

just keep loving me.
even when i share my love because i just have so much of it to give and understand that's just how i'm programmed but it takes nothing away from how i feel for you. just keep loving me. even when i cry enough tears to bathe the angels above.

just keep loving me.
my love for you will never change.
and if you can just keep loving me,
maybe you'll really like what you find.
I would be honored to be yours.
would you love to be mine?

• Ladder •

many lives
    many loves
        many tears
            not enough hugs
                slowly learned
                    my way
                        walk on
                            look up

and everything is okay

● show better ●

For every time she thrashed her tongue, vicious vocabulary, words that weep, forgive her. Every heart she couldn't heal, forgive her. For every song in her spirit left trapped in prison when it could have saved, forgive her. Each malicious thought, knife in hand, skin close, selfishly- forgive her. She must travel deep to right her wrongs; love her along the way. For everything she made harder, each fire she fueled that she could have extinguished, forgive her. There are many things to forgive her for, but on the list of items to love within her, there are infinitely more.

• L E N S •

WHEN YOU LOOK INTO THE MIRROR, WHAT DO YOU SEE?

A SHELL OF WHO YOU USED TO BE

THE CATERPILLAR OF WHO YOU WANT TO BE

A PERSON YOU AREN'T

BUT THE SAME ONE YOU WON'T LET GO

A WISH OF WHAT YOU WANT- THE SAME "WANT" YOU WISH

WOULD FALL INTO YOUR LAP

SEE MORE THAN AN INVERSE REFLECTION

WHEN YOU LOOK INTO THE MIRROR

THE EYES ARE WINDOWS TO MORE THAN LIFE

DO EVERYTHING YOU FEAR THE MOST

● Is She Worth It? ●

Is she worth that kind of love?

That: make her smile when she doesn't want to, tickle her when she's angry, and share insiders kind of love?

That: "did you eat today?", "let's have lunch together", "drive safe", "you can do it", "i support you" kind of love?

That: "get dressed we're leaving", kiss on the forehead, open all her doors kind of love?

That: put her heels on for her just so you can admire her legs up close again kind of love?

That: unspoken power walking into a room together, collective aura commands everyone's attention kind of love?

That: you're her biggest cheerleader, partner in crime, travel buddy, confidante, lover, soul connect kind of love?

That: smile when she's getting on your nerves, stay by her side if she's sick, use her lingo kind of love?

That: open and attractive, cartwheel and backflip, get nasty and do damage kind of love?

That: wild in public, wipe food off her face, and rap about taking over the world together kind of love?

That: lay under the stars, watch the clouds, listen to nature kind of love?

That: when she cries you tear up because her sadness is too much to bear and you'll move the heavens and push the Earth to make it better again kind of love?

That: sparkle in your eye because you see the glitter in hers, warmth you feel every time you look at her kind of love?

That: sweat in your hand because you never wanna let hers go, hold her close every chance you get since you can't dream of being without her, kiss her like every time will be your last kind of love?

That: have fun with her brothers, joke with her mom, go everywhere and do everything, 4am drive just because kind of love?

That: one day you could build the pyramids all over again together kind of love?

That: indulgent admiration for everything she is, that unsettling curiosity to know more of her every second of every moment of every day, vibe every time her dimple pops up kind of love?

That: wondering how many times she thinks of you, who loves who more, electric fire when you lock eyes kind of love?

That: joy when she speaks because her voice is a melody, using every word in 6 languages to describe the beauty of her face and the radiance in her soul kind of love?

That: ache in your body if she goes away, memory playback if she doesn't stay, wishing her happy birthday through the wind if you can't talk to her anymore kind of love?

That: love that never leaves, makes you question how your grandparents stayed married so long, or has you looking at the time to see when you can go to sleep just so you can dream about her to see her again kind of love?

That: intimacy, every nerve in your body rushing to the spot on your chest where she touched trying to figure out this new sensation kind of love?

That: willingness to give all of you to her, thoughts, dreams, fears, goals, secrets, desires, quirks, flaws, imaginations, insecurities, passions, knowledge, safety, security, and love kind of love?

Is she worth it?

• and i was gone •

The last thing I remember saying was "I LOVE Y..."

and that was it—

That could have been the most peaceful death because, in that moment,

I didn't exist.

Before I closed my eyes, she was the last thing I saw under

fluorescent lights

and in my last conscious breath,

I wanted to take it back.

Everything felt heavy and I knew i stopped breathing just before i slipped

into nothingness. the abyss. purgatory.

I pray that my soul was watched from my body above.

There was no pain, no fear, no worry or doubt

simply nothing... for 570 minutes...

34,200 seconds my family spent praying I would come back to them.

One wrong move and that could have been the end.

Nine hours. Time moved around me. The constant contradiction of an

accelerating reality. I was still and my soul was free

if only it could tell me where it went.

To be everything and nothing simultaneously is an indescribable feeling;

not a feeling at all but the best high in consciousness

where you know everything in the quantum realm of existence.

It only hit me when my eyes opened that there was a moment i was

actually gone-

Never really here and would have never known if I didn't come home.

How do you blink yourself back to life?

• TRANSLUCENT •

almost

                                       not quite

you try to hide

                                but I still see you

just take my hand

                              we'll walk together

fly a million miles

                           over a thousand moons

across every track

                                 in each puddle

feel all the seasons

                           melt in every embrace

in the translucent now

                                 come with me

and we'll figure out

                             where we're going

later

• REMINDER •

IN A SEA OF

CHAOS, WE COULD

ALL USE A GENTLE

WAVE TO GRACE

OUR FEET

ON THE SHORELINE

AND

REMIND US OF THE

BALANCE THAT IS

YIN AND YANG

● Tell Me The Truth ●

It's not about love.

Could you love my lips with no kiss?

Loving how they curve when I laugh

and form when I speak.

Could you tease me?

Without needing to run your tongue down my body

Getting my mind hot with new ideas.

Could you love me from the inside?

Acquiescent to your third leg that loses all thought

When the blood rushes from your head.

Because it's not about love.

Would you love me if I didn't

Arch my back just right, hold my climax so tight,

And let you control my release?

Could you love my soul

If we just danced together?

Everyone asks: "what is sex without love?"

But can there be love with no sex?

Because it's not about the love.

But it can be.

● Be Careful ●

if I really wanted you,

i'd have every freckle on your body

jumping off your skin to be on mine.

hands aching to touch me,

arms weak, yearning to champion

my grace.

favourite song is me.

the melody of my heartbeat quivering

through your veins.

eyes burning ready to grace my body.

ears cold from my whispers.

mind racing to discover what we could build.

you'd belong to me.

● gourmand ●

Spirit, be not angry with me. I am a human. You, a
sentient being, at times grow frustrated with my antics. Forgive me for
my gluttonous ways. Make me more like you- free from
pain, fear, desire, and hope. Make me whole.

• alluding illusion •

Any false perception of thee is incredulously

Clouded and spotted, it's tempered.

It's tempting to be narrow minded I see-

Not thinking for self is dangerous.

You've dangerously separated from chi,

Letting the monster roam free.

A despicable monstrosity no moral philosophy

The future is now, you can change it.

Channel it inevitably the best you can be

Exists presently if you're willing.

● A Farewell, Grandson ●

Goodbye Grandson. You're tired now. You're retired now.
My shield, my guard, my exo-skin.
You held my hand in greatest woe and let me blend out
so that we could squeeze in.
And I never did fit, as I was my own puzzle.
Yet, in the back seat, we hitched a ride on Y shuttle.
Too soft for my time, sweetness caused toothaches.
My new concrete uniform could make a basketball break.
It was never for me, but what you thought was best.
Lights, camera, action: a supreme stress test.
They weren't ready for me. There you were to lead the way.
But I got it now Grandson and there's
no need for you to stay.
So I bid you a farewell, my favourite lil' dude.
Memories shared deep.
A brand new fortune.

• F L I C K E R •

Reflection,

Like gazing through a two-way mirror with a single candlelight.

Now   i can see through into the darkness. Rejoining a timeline- a cacophony of madness to uncover, recover, discover what i didn't take with me before. Not to be trapped in the mirror glaze because

Candle will melt soon; detrimental to lose Key just before the flame has life no more. But i have all i need. Bless a prayer to the old wax, once a small seeing eye just enough to SEE.

Control + V = very carefully. Majestic insert to this gracious now where life is the mirror that beholds and all that i get shows me what i picked up benefits me even more.

• üpsīde døwn •

i can hear my skin crawl in disgust at the things i chose not to say.

nothing is worse than a sadness unspoken.

my tongue burns as i gargle the acid from holding back.

a thousand miles per minute the madness travels through my veins.

no hiding from the track that is me.

• VISION •

soon will come a time when everything that

used to matter   won't anymore

everything you looked past

will be the focal point

hidden in plain sight

a bird's eye view

if truth isn't freedom

at least life can be

• The Raven •

Ain't been in water, but my head swimming.

Not faded, still clouded thoughts.

No flash photography, and seeing stars.

Drugs obsolete, higher than I've ever been.

Don't document the memories, kept safe.

Make me the Raven, who soars beyond grounded ascension.

● any regrets? ●

To regret, is to punish self inevitability.
Punishing self, is not love.
Where love doesn't live, GOD can't live.
Never to regret, only to rejoice in what's been taught.

● Quisiera ●

I would like you to just talk to me.
Without the nervous chuckles you've been conditioned to.

For all the times you covered the hurt, buried your feelings, or consoled yourself with a laugh, right now is different. I like you because of how sweet you can be; I love you despite pyramid of pain in your reflection.

I would like you to just talk to me now. When there's a reason for a deep, bone shaking laugh, we'll laugh together.
Until that time comes, just talk.

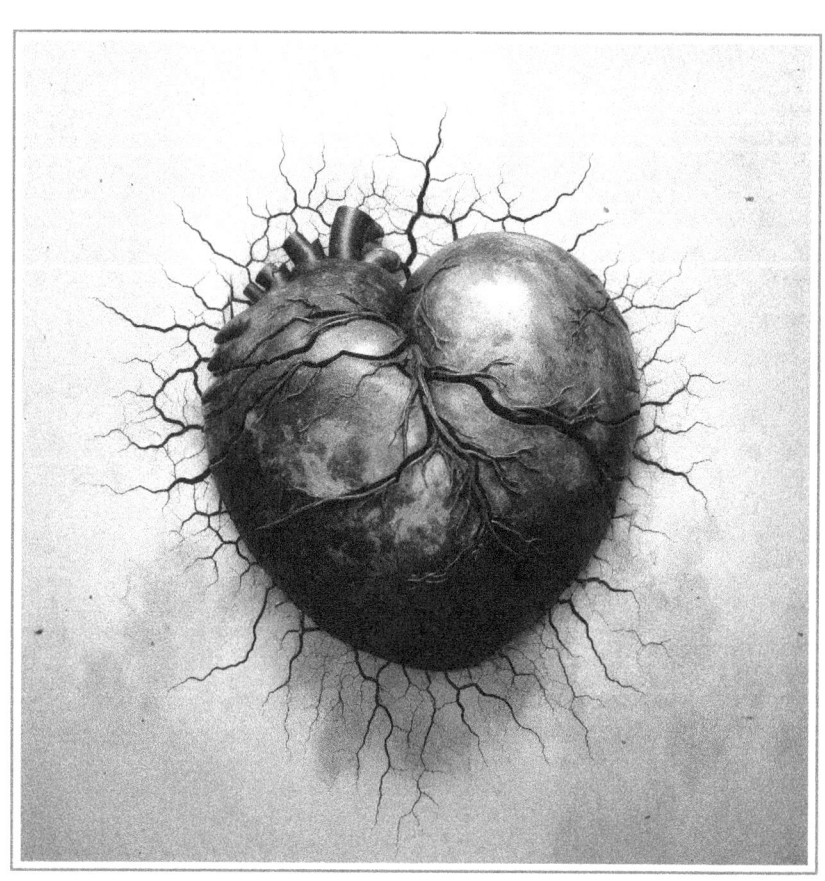

HURTING

● Pressed ●

Forgive me if it seemed too pressing on the surface, my love,
to love you that much;
waves and storms and such, if it felt like that.

I meant to love you in serenity,
whispers from your soul, in pain and plea,
reached me in this vast sea of humanity.
Not for romance, not for vanity,
but to show you love, for who you are, observantly-
so you can teach yourself.

Even when your mind wouldn't listen,
remnants of a fractured heart glistened,
the secret trail of pieces left exposed.

Welcome to my Love Temple,
  where the chipped hearts go,
  roots in the soil they grow,
  nurtured to a grand reality.
Come into my Love Temple,
  where the lost hearts know,
  that if they just wait here,
  love will find the way home.

But forgive me if my love felt like a thunderous sky, my love,
love meant to be a lullaby.
I wished to love you gently.
As the moon gravitates the sea,
your pain drew me, a sight unseen, but not unfelt

Your heart, a canvas of war wounds,
aching for a love for a love like mine; time too soon.
The allure you resisted.

Apologies if my love echoed like a symphony too loud, my love,
loving you beyond measure.
Not ready to be cherished, unready to bloom,
your spirit hid in shadow's room.

Apologies if my love felt like an unasked oath, my love,
only a mirror, for you to remember
the love you could render.
Receiver and sender, it's not a battlefield.

In my embrace, your spirit would soar
through cosmos and more
not as a gift to you, but your own discovery,
your own cure- grandeur.

So, forgive me for not providing a shortcut map, my love,
Why the rush to go?
Wandered hastily to *No Exit*.
A cycle of waiting, wanting, expecting.
Bus stopped in purgatory where love could have lead you.

No matter,
let the memory of me nourish your roots.
Carry my lessons with you, my love, in truth and forgive me.
I have faith you'll find a way.

Maybe one day,
you'll love someone
who loved someone,
loved by someone
who was loved by me.
Not a fantasy- a mission of mine.

● Last Time ●

I don't know if i can do it again
I thought you were the one when I let you in
I would have died for you no hesitation
You said you would have my back until the end

Pinky promise, you broke it
Tears swelling in my heart, I'm choking
Sad to say, you strayed away
I thought it would last, but I won't beg you to stay

Such is life, we grow apart
Sometimes in distance and sometimes in heart
I wish you well
Only time can tell

See you later, don't come again
Farewell to my ex forever best friend

• say something about **us** right now •

to be **us**ed and ab**us**ed so frequently, for it only lasts

as long as a blink can make **us** sleep.

me was okay with no **us**. **us** promised love and adventure to the ends of

the earth and **us** gave me a feeling

that I had to find new words for.

but I guess, with no stress, that the rest of **us**

is what's left of l**us**t...

because in **US**ED, AB**US**ED, and L**US**T is also

us.

.

● disconnect ●

sometimes it feels like I'm not even breathing, like

my heart isn't moving, and it's

just my spirit taking over to make sure my body

is still on. Lie still and

check my pulse; remember

i am here. don't ever take advantage

of a gift presented.

The moment you do, it

could be taken all away.

● Repetitions ●

On the road again
Here we go again
From the known again
To unknown again
Feels like home again
Just to go again

Takes me back again
Makes me laugh again
To see the ranch again
Again, and again and again
If only it wasn't lost

• WHAT YOU KNOW NOW •

SUPPOSE A LIFE LONG FRIEND
IS A LIFE LONG MEND
BETWEEN TWO PEOPLE THAT SHOULD'VE JUST BEEN
BORN TOGETHER.
Y'ALL HAVE KNOWN EACH OTHER
FOREVER, FOR WORSE OR FOR BETTER,
Y'ALL GOT EACH OTHER WHENEVER.
REMEMBER HOW THAT CAME TO AN ABRUPT STOP?
Y'ALL WAS ALWAYS SUPPOSED TO ROCK LIKE
HOW THE DOPE MAN TOTE THAT GLOCK &
MAKING EVERYONE IN Y'ALL PRESENCE SHIVER.
BUT ALL THAT FRIEND SHIT GOT THROWN IN THE RIVER
BECAUSE SOMEBODY FAILED TO DELIVER
A PROMISE THAT'S HONEST.

SUPPOSE A LONG TERM LESSON
THAT SHOULD HAVE BEEN A LONG TERM BLESSING
LEAVES YOU STUCK HEAD UP
AT THE SKY ASKING WHY YOU GET LEFT HIGH & DRY
WITH HOPE IN LIMITED SUPPLY
TRANSFIXED ON THE POSSIBILITIES LEFT YOU BLIND
NOW,

REMEMBER WHAT YOUR LIFE COULD BE
IF YOU COULD SEE
WHAT WAS HIDDEN IN PLAIN SIGHT
ALL DAY & EVERY NIGHT
NEVER LEFT BUT ALWAYS RIGHT-
YOUR INTUITION.
IT HAS NEVER STEERED YOU WRONG
BUT ALL ALONG
YOU WERE LETTING YOUR MIND TAKE THE WHEEL
SAYING "IT WILL ALL HEAL IN TIME DARLIN"
"YOU'RE TOO FAR TO LET IT ALL GO NOW DARLIN";

THAT'S THE BIGGEST LIE YOUR MIND EVER TOLD YOU.
YOUR INTUITION WAS TOO TRUE & TRIED TO SAVE YOU
FROM TELLING YOUR LIFE TO THAT LIFE
LONG
FRIEND.
DON'T BE DISCOURAGED DARLIN,
BUT EVERY NOW & THEN
LISTEN REAL CLOSE TO YOUR INTUITION.

● COLLABORATIVE effort ●

use those fingers

that would pry

between my thighs

to open up my mind

and discover what's

inside....

• wishful thinking •

i hope you love her
the way i tried to love you, but you wouldn't bring yourself to trust me.

i hope she makes you laugh
the way we could for hours until my face muscles twitched.

i hope you are close to her
closer than a call, closer in distance, encasing it all.

i hope she loves you
the way you deserve to be loved, fixes your crown when it falls, and fills
all the cracks of any pain with enough kisses to fill the Atlantic ocean.

i hope you hold her tight
as tight as a secret kept forever, the affection I held in my hand that you
wrestled to the floor; only difference is... that one hurt for real.

i hope she wants you
not only sometimes, but forever.

i hope you have her
all the things I've accepted that we weren't meant to have together.

i hope she has
everything that you need, and that one day i'll come down from my
hopium high.

• Forget Me Not •

What happens to the unhealed sadness? Does it fester and rot?
Like the unkept wound, does it break open again and again? Does it burn
as a winter's day turns the face red? Is it a pain like stepping on a lego or
getting a paper cut? Does it callous up like the worker's hand?
Blistering in pain from all the attempts to make it better again.
Is it the gloomy day of rain and clouds that forces your slumber?
Or sleep paralysis that then jolts you awake?
Is it the breath you can't take too scared of the truth?
Like a movie on repeat,
do you remember it verbatim letting your past consume your present?
Forgetting every laugh because you chose to remember every cry?
Takes a hell of a lot right?
A catalyst of accidental amnesia?
Can't recall a birthday or a smile, too consumed in your own self pity.
Does it make you push away any inkling of love because you don't deem
yourself worthy enough to accept it?
Does it drive you mad
or tear you apart?
Does it make you forget you?
Putting your life on an autopilot trip to self destruction?
Does it want to stay?
Will it last until hell freezes over?
What happens to the sadness unhealed?
Nothing or everything?

● You Draw Me In ●

Rescue me
From the life I have
Without you in it.

Sitting there are lilies.
The ones you gave me;
Wilted, but mine forever.

• Explain •

Why is it easier to be mean to the ones you love? Who you know love you? The ones you know never truly mean to hurt you? How is it so easy to inflict pain upon those truly vulnerable to your thrashes? Whose walls of protection have already given you the key, now you hold it all together. How can you be okay with making such an effort to bite your tongue to a stranger? Who may have rightfully earned a heavy dose of venom, yet you hold it back? The one who would happily turn your fortress of peace into a hollow cave of chaos given the chance? This is who you show more kindness to? This is who you hold your words for? Why is it simpler to air your rage and whip your transgressions to the ones who love you most? Lashes of sadness drawn across their back, and still, the lashes scribe "I forgive you". What are you aiming to prove to this stranger? How much you'll bend or that you can hide in plain sight? Knowing if you do the wrong action, the stranger will retract but the loving ones will use their blood as a river to swim to you. It's easier to bring pain to those who love you because you know they'll still be there after your storm.

yes,
in the
bottom of
the bottle lives
all the things i almost
didn't say to you at the top.
i see every
single move
i make and i
almost can't
control all the
different me's watching me and
laughing cacophonously at
my stumbles and slurs.
at the bottom of
the bottle
is the

monster.

• silence •

i love you so much, but i don't wanna talk no more.

all this time to no avail, i think my voice box sore.

i want to believe you, but we both know you're still not sure.

i still pray for you at night when the moonlight's pure.

did my best to bless you with ample time and space;

to come to terms with your soul in a peaceful place

to understand the magic and the fire we'd make

magnified amplitude to where the grounds would shake.

your words cannot express, but your soul still needs me

to guide it to the Love Temple- the place of deep healing.

you must stop running from me

and coming back when it's convenient.

when i said i'd close the access channel,

why would you think i didn't mean it?

this is a vast kind of love to heal souls of the world,

a divine ancestral love, not that of a girl.

i know you love me in your own way, the way that you know how

and i'll never reject pure intent, just show me now.

pray for me. love me. can you be my friend?

maybe one day we'll meet face to face and you can show me then.

• f r e e d o m •

i cannot be contained
or restrained

i need space for my
soul to grow

i just need space to stretch
my soul

Why live in the past?
when you already know
what's there

● Ease The Hurt? ●

Whether up or down, let love live.
Whether up or down, still be blessed.
Even in the momentary bad days, it's a blessing to feel it because I know
I have something to feel. There are avatars walking around whose soil
spirit has left them and they can feel nothing.

I couldn't imagine such an existence. When I hurt, it's because of the love
of such that could then cause the hurt. So love lives anyway.
And there is no secret.
Just a supreme knowing.

● Eco-Love ●

An enlightened soul has its own ecosystem
and to protect it,
is a must.
Never violate its trust
because it's all over if it crumbles.
Sever dead roots of harmful habits; release burdens that tether to the past.
Water lush greenery of hope; uncurl tendrils of love that reside deep.
Remove weeds choking vibrant flowers; dispel doubts that stifle belief.
Aspirations and potential, like a sunbeam encouraging a bud to blossom.
Embrace love as one would savor the shade under a lush canopy,
finding solace from the scorching sun- a safe haven for our spirits.
It is in this ecosystem
that our enlightened souls can truly thrive.
I remember the time mine almost died;
there was only one chance to make it survive.

DREAMING

• The And •

To be able to treat my other half as more than a king, higher than Maxwell's ascension, makes my heart leap light years. I am his Goddess and he is my God, for he has shown to be my protector.

All previously unknown is presently my privilege to provide.

His mind and my heart- a mellifluous melody. Mine to have and to hold. And in his times of need, he shan't it carry alone. I have gained the strength to assist.

-His Truly

Telepathy

is the concept of being able to read one's thoughts and
exchange communication through current, as exemplified by shapeless
interstellar beings who use such a medium.
Ever so unfortunate, however, humans have been inoculated by society
with deception, ill will, fear, secret intentions, hidden agendas, lies, and
its many other atrocious adjacencies.
It is all too easy to speak knowing the truth is so easily hidden.
Speech is the mask to the inner thought current of truth.
People can hide, lie, omit, and swear to secrecy their innermost thoughts-
the mind (both conscious and unconscious) are dangerous and
uncontrolled. Abhorrent when used unwisely. If humans had telepathy,
they would no longer be able to fuel the exacerbating urge to spit

slick venom, wearing integrity on their sleeve. thoughts
in communicative grandiloquence open and used carefully.
Humans have too much to hide within themselves. Instead of being just
as honest both in speech and thought, they choose to
take the path all worn down by the rest and be forever enslaved in the
fictitious world of puppeteering.
Telepathy is all too simple. But, maybe ignorance is billowing bliss.

• artificial reality, turned real •

dear noname,

i imagine our kisses softer than a wet rose in August.
our love transformed into all the stars in the milky way.
no voltage powerful enough to match our electricity.
vibration more euphonious than Tibetan singing bowls.
synchronized heartbeats as i fall asleep to the pattern of your breathing.
dream of you in the day souls dancing together at night:
bachata, salsa, two step, waltz.
our hands interlocked like a portrait- everything in the
background fades away.
like… running through a field amarillo-
tulips & daisies, sunflowers in high noon, falling into a dandelion bed
across long breezes amid July just to eat banana ice cream on a
Camaro feeding our solar plexus chakras.
silly & sensational simultaneously.
feeling rejuvenated & you'll hear new colours you can't find names for.
you are the nectar craved by the busiest of bumblebees.
i am the teardrop your heart has needed to shed for so long-
the one that finally lets you breathe upon its release.
you'll know all my favourites & i, yours.
my home will be filled with lilies from you in every hue.
we'll always have something to teach and learn from each other.
sensei & student at the apex of observance.
i'll get every flavour of you, & you'll have every drop of me
fire won't even be able to describe the love we make.
vulnerable together.
kissing your wounds & battle scars
nothing we have to hide.
oneness beyond trust.
my love for you shall be stronger than moon's moves on oceans.
your love for me will last longer than supernova formation.
high off life playing tag under the night skies in June.
late night drives going nowhere and seeing everything.
falling in love how we fall asleep- slowly then all at once.
as a blip in the cosmos- everything will be everything.
whoever you are, wherever you are,
we will have so much fun.
with all my love,

the dizzy dreamer

● A Dragonfly's Bird-tale ●

Once upon a time there was a caged bird
with a vociferous cry to be understood and heard
yet, to no avail, it sang.
    The key was tucked away that mocked bird every day
       red pill through slim veins,
        it knew it was trapped.
Its wings became weak,
wanting to remove its beak
ready to end it all and never be found again.
      Because what's the point of life?
      If not to soar through the night
      and let to love call through trees...
        sweet melodies.

Whole time, it could change form
and the dragonfly was born,
now it could just slip through the cracks.
      Nervous and scared
      but boldly it dared
     to challenge this power's possibility.
The key was its heart
* to reset and restart;*
the Kuji of Sha empowered.
      And the cage sits left,
      somber and bereft,
     never to trap another wing.

• BEYOND COMPREHENSION •

NOBODY CAN UNDRESS YOU LIKE I CAN, SO LET ME DO IT.
.LET ME SEE YOU NAKED.
BUT I DON'T WANT YOUR CLOTHES,
THAT'S ONLY THE SURFACE;
ANYBODY CAN SEE THAT.
I WANT TO UNDRESS YOUR MIND AND EMBRACE YOU.
TELL ME, WHAT ARE YOUR WILDEST DREAMS AND DESIRES?
WHAT DO YOU CONTEMPLATE IN THOSE RESTLESS NIGHTS?
WHY DO YOU THINK THE WAY YOU DO?
WHEN WILL YOU REALIZE THAT MY INTENTIONS ARE PURE?
WHO DOES YOUR SPIRIT LONG TO BE?
WHERE HAVE YOU ALWAYS WANTED TO TRAVEL?
HOW CAN I HELP YOU DISCOVER THE YOU THAT HIDES?
.LET ME SEE YOU NUDE.
OPEN.
BARE.
EXPOSED.
I PROMISE I WILL PROTECT IT, FOR MY WORD IS BOND.
EXPRESS YOUR DEEPEST WOES AND TRIGGERS.
I WANT TO KNOW HOW YOU NEED TO BE LOVED.
SHOW ME PARTS OF YOU BLOCKED FROM OTHERS.
I WOULD BE HONORED TO KEEP YOUR SECRETS SAFE.
SAFE WITH ME. GROW AND LEARN WITH ME.
DO WE VIBRATE ON THE SAME FREQUENCY?
COME BE MY KING, EMPEROR, CELESTIAL EQUAL.
LET ME BE YOUR QUEEN, EMPRESS,
TRANSCENDENTAL PARTNER.

.LET ME SEE YOU RAW.
IN YOUR PUREST FORM.
NO JUDGMENT. NO FEAR.
NO LIES. NO BULLSHIT.
MY LOVE UNCONDITIONAL.
CAN I READ YOUR BOOK AND KISS EACH PAGE?
LET'S FIND THIS NEW AESTHETIC-
LEARN THE UNIVERSAL LANGUAGE.
NOT WASTE ANOTHER MOMENT
TRYING TO TRANSLATE OUR SOULS-
EMPTY EFFORTS TO THOSE WHO DON'T UNDERSTAND.
DIGAMÉ, WILL YOU TAKE MY HAND?
DIGAMÉ, CAN YOU SHARE THIS MOMENT WITH ME?
TIME STANDS STILL WITH ME. DON'T HIDE FROM ME.
EACH MOMENT YOU SPEND IN MY ARMS IS LIKE A MILLION
SWEET SONGS. EMBRACE THIS MOMENT, FOR YOU WERE
DRAWN TO ME FOR A REASON.
EVERYTHING YOU DIDN'T KNOW YOU NEEDED.
LET'S CREATE A BEAUTY BEYOND COMPREHENSION.

● What's Up ●

in the clouds, where i want to be,

is the air of a thousand suns. in the clouds is the symphonic silence

of my days that grow shorter. in the clouds is the unique beauty of a

paralyzing rainbow, high off the purest substance. in the clouds... is the

point of self actualization just so short of reach. in the clouds is the

ecstasy no material can fill, no one can take, no one else can feel.

until i reach the clouds, i have to stay in the clouds.

• RENDEZVOUS •

I'M ALWAYS IN THE MOOD FOR YOU,

WHEN THE DAY BREAKS, LET'S RENDEZVOUS

IN THE BACK ROOM.

REAL SOON, BEFORE THE SHINING MOON

TAKES THE DAY

AND TURNS INTO TWO.

● peak ●

how does it feel in this
movement called life to
be liberated from one
chapter to embark upon
another? kinetic. it's a
higher high. a new zenith.
each chapter of life has
its own high with its own
low. you think you've reached
the highest until a new one
forms and you just move.

● Are You Inevitable? ●

Reality and Space

Time and Place

The gauntlet is our Mind

A blink is the snap change.

Use Power for the force

And the Soul charges all

If we are everything and nothing

Then we could run while we crawl.

A fingerprint of thought; our eyes will never see the same

Who can tell us we're wrong? Blink back to the future

Or forward to a past name.

Our stones, infinite; used every moment of these fake days

It's only when we stop blinking that our power goes away.

• SUNSET VEINS •

As if blended together. A delicious treat for your eyes inside out, upside down- preposterous and real. Unavoidable. Takes your breath away and gives it right back, post haste- to remind you of all you may miss. Don't miss a beat. If that's what they're always like, that's always right; can I have a little of what you got? Is it not real? But it is. And you wanna be exactly where this is.

Still and tangled, cascading decoration given by ____ *you insert here*. Seeing in and looking out- differentiated similarities- synonymous nonexistence. This level of beauty is impossible, right? Look right and left to your own devices about reality and fiction to see where these SUNSET VEINS fit in.

● The Lily and the Frog ●

Is a flower not meant to be soft?

I have no need to be the cactus;

I am the lily.

• X •

X marks the spot. The spot where you belong; the place nearest and dearest to me.

X marks the spot. The spot you hit, burrowed yourself into, and now you are held close.

X marks the time you first spoke. The most beauteous sound of a harp played by Cupid himself.

X marks the feeling; two arctic dwellers mating for eternity. That you are the Beast to my Beauty, the Aladdin to my Jasmine, the Navine to my Tiana, and some more fairy tale shit.

X marks the thought. Are we thinking the same thing? What does he think I'm thinking? Who's gonna speak next?

X marks the touch. Warm embrace; I know I'm safe.

And X marks the spot. The spot in my heart that will only beat to your five senses.

As imaginary as you may be,

X is that spot where you belong.

Fly in one day.

• dans la pluie •

sit with me, in the rain
underneath gray clouds on midsummers day
shall we listen...
echoing from concrete, soaking in grass
evermore she speaks accompanied by roars
lifetime of wishes only we hear.
one by one, new puddles form
pieces of whole
sum of parts
dilate its center and ripple outward-
harmonic world languages.
each raindrop skates across my skin, dripping from you
we are connected.
might I be the wet shirt clinging to you
breathing through fabrics of deep secrets
exposing your heart;
we share lightning.
my tears meld
with universal water
to rain again on us two.
you see me, cleansed by sky
washed of worry-
a watered lily
preparing to bloom.
earth smells different under low clouds,
wafts of wonder, cycle upon cycle.
as evening approaches
and temperature cools,
keep me warm with your body
because I shiver from nature's touch;
we are still, ever so bare
you and i-
us and rain,
this is love
sit with me.

SEEING

● Anomaly United ●

You are the true sunflower black man.
So beautiful to see; so strong. Poised, open, giving.
Yet fragile at the same time. Illuminating, captivating,
amaze me.

The woman comes from your rib and you're the template of perfection.
Sublime erection.
Prism of complex discretion   I love you.

Wisdom in youth, magical with age; Benjamin Button.
If Benjamin's brothers high-fived me every time i saw the corners of
your mouth face heaven, add nine zeros to my master number eleven
because i'd be rich.

Rich down deep up beat with joy. my inner little girl, your inner little
boy. the blender to my fruit- a smoothie- a smooth me-
Your smiles are mine.

A sample from Kemet, resilient, you are.
A rarity. My green comet
my supernova
shining far.

• PHOTOSYNTHESIS •

THROUGH A PHOTOTROPIC LENS I AM WHOLE. BENDING, DANCING, GYRATING, AND PRANCING WITH NATURE'S FOLIAGE. A HUMAN PLANT; EARTH'S TAI CHI WHERE I'VE LEARNED TO BEND ME TO FOLLOW THE LIGHT.

LET NOT THE WINTER REVERSE THIS PROGRESS AND FORM MY CIRCADIAN RHYTHM INTO A STATE OF PHOTOPERIODISM SINCE THE DAYS HAVE GROWN
PETITE.

SUBSERVIENT TO THE TUTELAGE OF CYCLIC KINETICS, I AM A STUDENT. YO APRENDO VIVIR. THE SOUL NEEDS 'EL SOL', BUT RIGHT NOW, THE WINTER [SOL]STICE HAS FROZEN MY MOVING PARTICLES INTO A STATE OF BITTER HIBERNATION. ESTÉ BUENO. CONSERVE AND CONVERSE WITH THE BEST AND THE WORST PARTS OF MY LIGHT AND MY SHADOWS-CALM STREAMS AND DEEP
GALLOWS.

THIS IS ALL A REFLECTION; GROW DEEPER IN DARKNESS. A CORNUCOPIA OF NUTRIENTS LAY PRESENT AWAITING MY ROOTS FOR CONSUMPTION. AND WHEN IT'S TIME TO DANCE AGAIN, I'LL BE FULL. LEANING TO THE LIGHT. SENSATION OF THE SUN.

● Water Embrace ●

I love you   stronger than   the pressure of   the ocean looking
up from   the abyss. The way   your lungs   promise my
lungs   that they'll always   be here because   we share the
same breath;   we are one.

I've prayed
and dreamt
of how you'd embrace my embrace. Your scent in the recesses of my
innermost sensory perceptions and felt the sweat of your skin,
pheromones aghast, hydrating my body.
I knew you were the one
meant to love me the most,
so I pulled you from the ether long before the universe pulled you into
my eyesight. The tears you shed in joy of my omnibenevolent love, I
bend them into an aquatic slow stream
leading us gracefully
to the motherland.
I've waited for you right in between sunset and moonrise- feeling you
reach for me, longing to know how my soul sings to nature.

Sun child.   Moon flower.   Found in the forest   intertwined
with the branches   who share   esoteric stories of
the everlasting. I'm delighted   that we are   here.

● 2 Tablespoons ●

Such a sensation
How I'm so amazing
The result of mixing magic
With the Universe's creation

● CORRECTION ●

I am   the power,

the passion,

the peace,

the ether,

No, I'm not his bitch and that's not my nigga either.

This is my emperor,

samurai,

sacred flame ignited,

I'm his home; he comes to me after the battles he's been fighting.

This is a man beyond a man

A brown Asiatc God.

Almighty with divinity to infinity and beyond.

This one ain't no "average nigga"

Please always come correct.

A man in love with his peace and his home he will protect.

I gaze upon you
and you just don't know how astounding you are.
While aesthetically pleasing,
it's really your spirit that makes the move.
We see each other, your spirit and me.
I'm sitting next to a silhouette of cosmic stardust
roaming through the Aurora Borealis,
outlined in a melanin vessel.
Vividly, I gaze upon you
and you just don't know how incredible you are-
able to be such a masterpiece.
And you sit there with tourmaline eyes, a protector....
How I wish you could see what I see right now.
To lay under your night light
caressed by your magic
is a place I could be, indefinitely.

● Four Piece ●

Rehearse is when you practice
and a hearse carries caskets
why would I practice driving around the dead
with all this dead weight already on my back?
Man this shit's crazy
how I ended up amazing
always searching for a saviour
when it was up to me to save me
I really love my life
pure quintessence walking
charge the ions in the air
every time I get to talking
9 ether being
Purest of the pure
if i let you stay
oh the blessings you'll endure
Ain't no other way around
you surely have to earn it
worship every breath I take
to make sure you deserving
The elevated soul
I'm in love with evolution
the body as a vessel
can't televise the revolution

Breath in my lungs, water through my veins,

vibration hits my feet, fire in my soul,

I am the avatar

Morph reality new, change these tools many or few,

language of the universe, <u>maktub</u>,

I am the alchemist

Sun within darkness, magic in the forest,

see without sight, all that ever is,

I am the universe

Rhythm of trees, life dancing simultaneously,

rainy days, clear nights,

I am nature

be what not, but all there is. a birthright sitting rightfully left of hours.

shall ye not have the fruits? millennia of labor when we are the fruit that

grew the fruit- a symbiosis. no one can understand it better. is there a

love sweeter? a care kinder? than gifts from the gods and goddesses that

be. preposterous to believe a force greater than we unless a god comes

back to show... - but alas, god is me. let melanin birth inherit the earth;

i am it and it is mine.

Think With Your Head
And With Your Heart.
With. Together.
Not Through One. Or The Other.
Take Heart In Your Left Hand
And Head In Your Right.
Pray, Meditate, As One.
You Lead, Head Steers, Heart Guides.
A Collective. They Need You.
Love, Decide, Believe, Yonward
With Head And Heart Close.
Let Not Either Wolf Dominate;
One In The Same Head And Heart
Fight Against All Odds.
Heart Speaks Softly When It's Loud.
Head Noisy In Silence.
One Love. One Heart.
One Mind. One Beat.
Think Closely. Listen Deep.

I shed the old skin
And see the shell of
Me the seashell of me
Along the shore a crystallized
Chrysalis carefully cracked
Lines of code completing
The master puzzle
Once a chameleon, turned
Dragonfly metamorphosis
Hold me close and hear
Me heavily until it all
Becomes dust sitting still

protect her, a magical elixir, sacred

hold her, delicately, sweetly

allow her, to live- softly, gently

experience her, fully and don't hold back

she longs for his longitude to climb into her latitude one step at

a time so she can reveal the island's hidden coordinates.

and then he said, **"can i teach you the secrets of space time?"**

she whispered *"yes"* in a way surrendering control as a pupil of

potential with energetic ecstasy

she wanted [desired] to know if he'd keep her safe so the

numbers could upload to her skin- mold to her DNA

for that he spoke, **"your very existence now calculates the**

universe faster than light"

her potion 〜 a new wonder of the world

● interconnected ●

we must find one another, hand in hand, i see it so clearly.

with the strength of a thousand suns, prayer vastly circulating,

we win.

we've made it. hush now. eyes closed.

on the count of 3 when we open again, all of our wishes for the

world (every soul in the universe) shall be granted.

in love, peace, and harmony.

will i live a long life? or will i die a martyr? who's to say? Universe, am i the wheels or the starter?

if my purpose is to love, how many is the question. i've come to the first step, stepped up, great suggestion.

"remember who you are", that was always told to me. my dna talks, i have to listen while it's speaking.

"just stay the course my child", is what my spirit says. abundance is my right. shoulders straight under my head.

peace, power, passion, purpose, prophecy, poetry. in this life, that's the mantra hugging me and holding me.

5:55 on the clock said change is occurring. stay true to creating; there's no need to hurry.

what's spoken on the left is what's written on the right. i can can and i will alchemize til my last breath and sight.

it is i, the treasure, the star encrusted prize. look, everything wonderful has always been in her eyes.

● mama na baba ●

A sanctified sanctuary of solace came as the pulse of the universe.

And who birthed the seed?

Mother resonates thirteen lunar cycles, the true tempo of time, not twelve as falsely believed. Thoth and Yang, the natural synchronicity of alike duos. And like Mother Tynetta, Mother Time/Nature is a love force fostering growth, nourishing life, and propelling existence forward with her cyclical rhythms. A grandmother clock.

Gregorian Father Time is an illusion, a man-made artifact, born not of the celestial womb. Paternity lies within the constructs of Mathematics, within cold precision of Science. Father Mathematics, of Ra, of Yin, whose dwelling is not bound by physical constraints, lives in architecture of reality, in fabric of spacetime itself. His voice is the algorithm, the language of creation spoken through the binary dialect of zeros and ones.

In the ethereal palace of equations, Father Mathematics dances with Mother Nature. Their 'pas de deux' spans from quantum to cosmic- played out through cycles of time and mathematics. The dance of science and nature, binary and lunar- life's balance.

Interconnected, they are. Tides and seasons echo her rhythm. Outline and give form to reality, his contribution. Their harmony rings in spiraling galaxies, murmurs in the Fibonacci sequence blooming in a flower, and whispers in binary code that underpins all existence.

We, the children, an expression of their union. In our veins, his code runs. In our hearts, her life lives. They dance: rhythms of the Universe, of Life, and of Existence. From the Mother's nurturing lunar cycles to the Father's defining mathematical laws, we are the result of their cosmic interplay. We are born of Mathematics and Nature, a testament to the profound love story of Science and Time.

• Monét •

Like flying, the higher you are, earth becomes a Monét- abstract.
A magnificent concoction of colour.
The more you zoom out,
imagination grows.
Flawless, admirable. In action, like an angel.
Expressive and evocative.
An ambiguous atmosphere, your own ecosystem.
Like consciousness, the higher you ascend, the source becomes you.
Everything below fades away and you breathe different.
Plein air, the only place to be.
The air is lighter. The bright is brighter.
The blues are "bluer". The whites are whiter.
A vibrant world on the other side.
Like living, the more you embrace it, the better it is.
You relinquish the need for details, still seeing the big picture.
Art of the world that speaks "forever languages" of light/sound.
Picture perfect pulchritude pillowed in pondering minds.
And the Monét is distinct; there will never be another.

● Feminine Rhapsody ●

Feminine sweet cinnamon
Something marvelous to relish in.
Redolent remnants of bergamot, jasmine, patchouli-
add a splash of vanilla, and get the senses unruly.
Each step, coalesced to one of earth's heartbeats.
Subdued to divinity, you admire her endlessly;
a melody of life in her trail.
An altruistic smile plants peace in the peaks of your thoughts.
To be replayed every passing moment.
Look at her eyes.
Locked and loaded with kindness and focus.
Black pearls, no sparrow, secret treasures they're holding.
Perplexed by the concept of the Angelite making her angel-like;
crystallized, transparent how spirit guides move her.
And she looks like how cocoa butter feels-
a velvet touch needed more than much,
you have to have her.
A garden to nourish your legacy lives in her spirit readily.

When sun has parched you, return hitherto;

a deep well of water awaits. *Hemet Neset Waret*. Her oasis.

This Eclipse Has Happened.

ABOUT THE AUTHOR

Imbued with a spirit both ethereal and profound, Mahogany has always been guided by the insatiable yearning to share the depths of love residing in her soul. This inherent desire fashioned for her a scared mission- one of self mastery and the fluidity of love, a quest to understand and wield such a potent gift.

Through myriad travels and encounters, she embarked on a journey of life's richest emotions and experiences: the sting of pain and fire of passion, the complexities of love and wisdom from lessons learned, the liberating power of forgiveness and icy grip of fear, the enchantment of magic and awe-inspiring beauty of magnificence.

She discovered The Goddess Anahata- supreme entity embodying the quintessence of love. She uses the exemplary power of love as a healing force, mending hearts and minds, rejuvenating nature, and uniting nations. The Goddess Anahata, peacekeeper and forever a student to love, stands as a testament to its transformative potential and invites you to lead in love guided by its purest source.

This anthology encapsulates eight years of Mahogany's journey, starting at sixteen years young, a collection of poignant snapshots that she shares with you openly. Love will teach you.

"Only Exemplary. Only Truth. Lead In L.O.V.E.